SIMPLY SCIENCE

Summer

by Darlene R. Stille

Content Advisers: Terrence E. Young Jr., M.Ed., M.L.S.,
Jefferson Parish (La.) Public Schools, and Janann Jenner, Ph.D.

Reading Adviser: Dr. Linda D. Labbo,
Department of Reading Education, College of Education,
The University of Georgia

 COMPASS POINT BOOKS
Minneapolis, Minnesota

Compass Point Books
3722 West 50th Street, #115
Minneapolis, MN 55410

Visit Compass Point Books on the Internet at *www.compasspointbooks.com* or e-mail your
request to *custserv@compasspointbooks.com*

Photographs ©:
Kent and Donna Dannen, cover, 4; Richard Hamilton Smith, 5, 27; Photo Network/Jim Schwabel, 6; ESA/TSADO/Tom Stack
and Associates, 7; Leslie O'Shaughnessy, 8; David Falconer, 10, 25; Jessie M. Harris, 11; Bill and Sally Fletcher/Tom Stack and
Associates, 12; Mark A. Schneider/Dembinsky Photo Associates, 13; Brian Parker/Tom Stack and Associates, 15, 28; Marilyn
Moseley La Mantia, 16; John Elk III, 19; John Shaw/Tom Stack and Associates, 20; Photo Network/Chad Ehlers, 21; Joe McDonald/
Tom Stack and Associates, 22; Doug Sokell/Visuals Unlimited, 23; Unicorn Stock Photos/Jeff Greenberg, 24; Jeff Greenberg/Visuals
Unlimited, 26; Unicorn Stock Photos/Tom MacCarthy, 29.

Editors: E. Russell Primm, Emily J. Dolbear, and Melissa Stewart
Photo Researcher: Svetlana Zhurkina
Photo Selector: Matthew Eisentrager-Warner
Designer: Bradfordesign, Inc.

Library of Congress Cataloging-in-Publication Data

Stille, Darlene R.
    Summer / by Darlene Stille.
      p. cm. — (Simply science)
    Includes bibliographical references and index.
    ISBN 0-7565-0095-8 (hardcover : lib. bdg.)
      1. Summer—Juvenile literature. [1. Summer.] I. Title. II. Simply science (Minneapolis, Minn.)
    QB637.6 .S75 2001
    508.2 —dc21   00-011004

Table of Contents

Summer Is a Season

What time of year do you like best? Is summertime your favorite? Do you go to summer camp? Do you go on trips? Do you go to the beach? Do you play outside all day?

Summer is one of the four seasons of the year. It comes after spring and before fall.

Fishing is especially fun in summer.

Eating ice cream in the summer heat

Summer is the warmest season of the year. You can go swimming, and you can wear shorts. Some summer days are cool though. And rainy days can come in summer too. Big summer storms can bring lightning, thunder, wind, and rain.

Beachgoers must be careful not to get too much sun.

The sun is made of gas.

The Summer Sun

Do you know what makes summer the warmest season? It is the sun. The sun is a huge ball of gas that gives off heat and light. Heat from the sun warms up the ground and the air too.

All life on Earth needs the sun. Light from the sun helps

plants to grow. When you eat lots of those plants, your body grows big and strong.

You could not survive without the sun, but its rays can hurt people. If you are not careful, the sun's rays can burn your skin. It's smart to wear a hat and sunglasses in the summer. It is also important to put **sunscreen** on your skin.

Sunscreen is important protection against sunburn.

Summer Days and Nights

What can you see on a warm summer day? You can see bees buzzing around the flowers and butterflies flitting through the air. You can see ducks swimming on ponds and watch frogs catching flies. You can see and hear the songbirds in the trees. What can you see on a warm

◀ Watching the sunset

Butterflies are a common ▶
sight during the summer.

summer night? You can see fireflies flashing in an open field and stars twinkling in the sky.

Look at the stars. Do some of them seem to form shapes? One shape is called the **Big Dipper**. Pretend you can draw lines to connect the seven stars in the Big Dipper. Your picture would look like a bowl with a long handle—a big dipper!

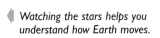
Watching the stars helps you understand how Earth moves.

The Big Dipper ▶

Watch the sky one night each week all summer long. Does the Big Dipper move? It may look like it moves, but stars do not move. It is Earth that moves. Earth travels around the sun. It takes one full year for Earth to go around the sun. Earth's motion makes it seem as if the Big Dipper moves to different parts of the sky.

At sunset, one part of Earth is moving away from the sun.

Why We Have Summer

Different parts of Earth tip, or **tilt**, toward the sun at different times of the year. That is why we have summer.

Pretend Earth is a big ball. Imagine a stick going right through its center. The stick goes in at the top of Earth

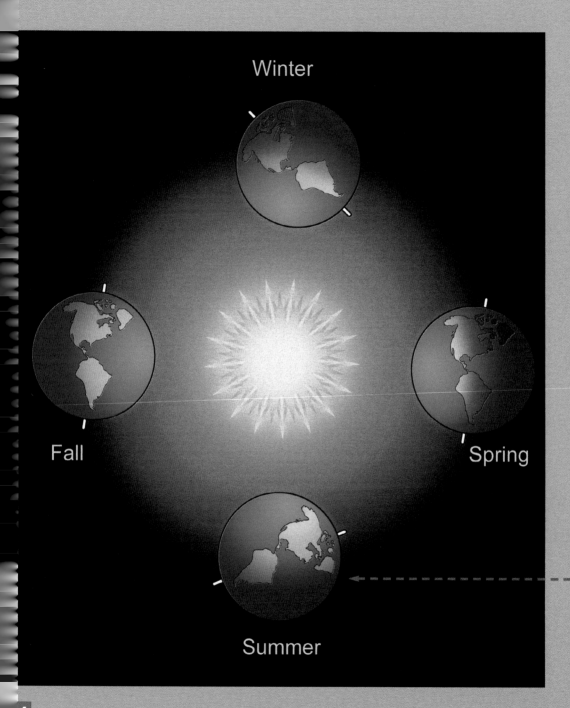

Winter

Fall

Spring

Summer

and comes out at the bottom. Earth has no stick going through its center, of course. But this idea helps you see how parts of Earth can be tipped toward the sun.

This imaginary stick is called an **axis**. Earth's imaginary axis is always tilted a little bit. The part of Earth that is tipped toward the sun gets the most heat from the sun.

During some parts of the year, the tilt makes the top part of Earth point toward the sun. During other parts of the year, the bottom part of

◀ Seasons occur as Earth travels around the sun.

Earth points toward the sun. It is summer on the part of Earth that is tipped toward the sun.

When the top half of Earth is tipped toward the sun, it is summer in North America, Europe, Asia, and northern Africa. When the bottom half of Earth is tipped toward the sun, it is summer in South America, Australia, southern Africa, and Antarctica.

Summer in Europe ▶

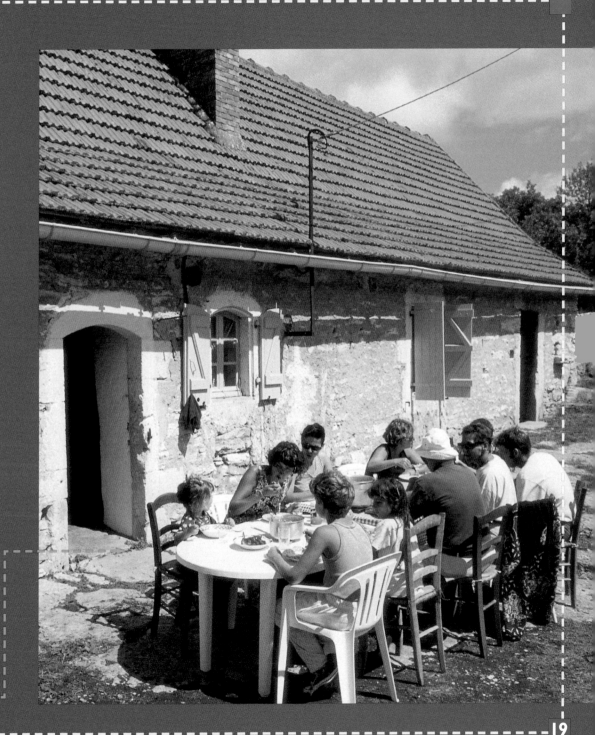

Hot As a Desert

In most parts of the world, some summer days are very hot, but others are just warm. In most **deserts**, however, summer days are always hot and dry. There is very little water in a desert. Only a few plants and animals can live there.

Cactus plants can live in a desert. The cactus can store water in its thick stem.

Blooming flowers in the Mojave Desert in California

Death Valley is a desert area in California

Many cactuses have sharp spines that keep animals away.

Kangaroo rats and many other desert animals stay cool by hiding underground during the day. They come out to look for food at night when it is cooler.

Some lizards, toads, insects, and other desert animals never go out in the heat. They sleep all summer long.

The Texas horned lizard is a desert animal.

Desert cactuses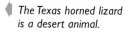

Always Summer

Some places on Earth stay hot all year round. These places are called the **tropics**.

Look at a globe to find the tropics. They are located just above and just below an imaginary line called the equator. The equator runs around the middle of Earth.

The tropics are never tilted away from the sun. So these areas are warm during every

◀ Miami, Florida, is warm all year round.

The Tropic of Cancer is close to Hawaii. ▶

season. Plants are green and flowers bloom all year long in the tropics. You can go swimming every day.

The tropics do not have four seasons like the rest of the world. They have just two seasons. They have a rainy season and a dry season. During the rainy season, it rains almost every day. During the dry season, it almost never rains.

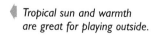

Tropical sun and warmth are great for playing outside.

Enjoying the summer while it lasts ▶

Summer Comes and Goes

In North America, the first day of summer comes around June 21. That day has more hours of daylight than any other day of the year. That means it also has the fewest hours of darkness. The days in July and August are

long too. You can play outside after you eat dinner. It might still be daylight when you go to bed!

By the time fall comes, you probably notice that the days are getting shorter. Night comes earlier and earlier.

Around September 21, the hours of daylight and darkness are equal. The day is twelve hours long, and the night is twelve hours long too. That is when summer ends and fall begins.

You can stay outside longer during the summer.

How do you know that summer is ending?

Glossary

axis—an imaginary line running through the center of Earth from the North Pole to the South Pole

Big Dipper—a group of stars that people think is shaped like a familiar object

cactus—a plant that can live in a desert

deserts—areas of land that are always dry and usually hot

equator—an imaginary line around the center of Earth

sunscreen—a cream that is rubbed on a person's skin to keep out some of the sun's harmful rays from entering the body

tilt—to tip

tropics—parts of Earth near the equator where the air temperature is about the same all year round

Did You Know?

- A day is the time it takes Earth to spin once on its axis. A day is twenty-four hours long. A year is the time it takes Earth to travel once around the sun. A year is about 365 days long.

- The two stars on the outer edge of the Big Dipper's bowl are called "pointers." If you follow the line that they make upward, you will see a bright star called the North Star. In the past, when sailors couldn't see land, they used the North Star to figure out where they were.

- Sunscreens protect your skin against only some of the sun's rays. That is why it is important not to spend too much time in the sun—even if you are wearing sunscreen.

Want to Know More?

At the Library

Ross, Kathy, and Vicky Enright (illustrator). *Crafts to Make in the Summer*. Brookfield, Conn.: Millbrook Press, 1999.

Sipiera, Paul P., and Diane M. Sipiera. *Seasons*. Danbury, Conn.: Children's Press, 1998.

Supraner, Robyn. *I Can Read about Seasons*. Mahwah, N.J.: Troll, 1999.

On the Web

Crafts for Kids

http://craftsforkids.about.com/parenting/craftsforkids

For dozens of craft projects related to the current season

Solstices and Seasons

http://geography.about.com/library/weekly/aa062397.htm

For information about the first day of summer, or summer solstice

Through the Mail

Farmers' Almanac Order Desk

P.O. Box 1609

Mount Hope Avenue

Lewiston, ME 04241

To order a seasonal guide with long-range weather forecasts

On the Road

Museum of Science

Science Park

Boston, MA 02114-1099

617/723-2500

To see exhibits that explore what causes the seasons, how Earth moves through space, and more

Index

About the Author

Darlene R. Stille is a science editor and writer. She has lived in Chicago, Illinois, all her life. When she was in high school, she fell in love with science. While attending the University of Illinois, she discovered that she also enjoyed writing. Today she feels fortunate to have a career that allows her to pursue both her interests. Darlene R. Stille has written more than thirty books for young people.